Nice or Nasty?

LEARNING ABOUT DRUGS AND YOUR HEALTH

WAYLAND

All Wayland books encourage children to read and help them improve their literacy.

✓ The page numbers and index can be used to locate a particular piece of information.

✓ The glossary reinforces alphabetic knowledge and extends vocabulary.

✓ The books to read section suggests other books dealing with the same subject.

First published in Great Britain in 1998 by
Wayland Publishers Ltd
This edition reprinted in 2002 by Hodder Wayland,
an imprint of Hodder Children's Books
Reprinted in 2003

Revised in 2007 by Wayland, an imprint of
Hachette Children's Books

Hachette Children's Books
338 Euston Road, London NW1 3BH

British Library Cataloguing in Publication Data
Llewellyn, Claire
Nice or Nasty? : learning about drugs and
your health. (Me and my body)
1. Substance abuse 2. Juvenile literature
I. Title II. Gordon, Mike 1948 –
362.2'9

ISBN 978 0 7502 5271 3

Printed in China

ME AND MY BODY series:
Am I Fit and Healthy?
LEARNING ABOUT DIET AND EXERCISE

Nice or Nasty?
LEARNING ABOUT DRUGS AND YOUR HEALTH

Where Did I Come From?
A FIRST LOOK AT SEX EDUCATION

Why Wash?
LEARNING ABOUT PERSONAL HYGIENE

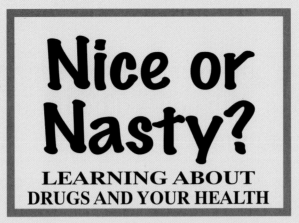

Nice or Nasty?

**LEARNING ABOUT
DRUGS AND YOUR HEALTH**

Written by Claire Llewellyn
and
illustrated by Mike Gordon

Have you ever had something
wrong with you – a bad pain in
your tummy ...

a sore, swollen throat ...

or an earache that really hurt?

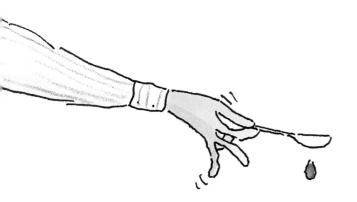

You probably had some medicine
from the doctor.

You were given the right dose, and in a day or two you soon started feeling better.

Some people have to take medicine every day.

That's because they have a condition that won't go away.

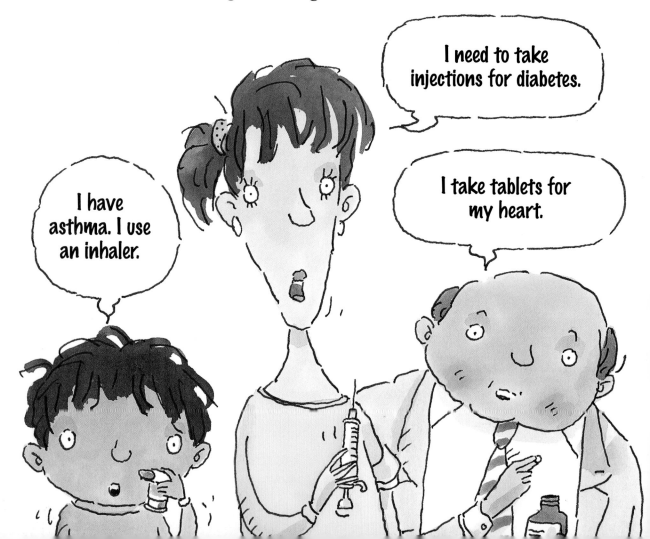

Their medicine makes
them feel comfortable
and well.

Did you know that another name for medicines is drugs?

Drugs work inside our body, and can help us in many different ways.

They can kill germs ...

.... calm a cough ...

or stop something really hurting.

Some drugs stop us catching
nasty diseases.

Others help to fight them if we do.

Drugs are so strong that we only need a
tiny dose.

In fact, too much of a drug can
be harmful.

It can make
you sleepy ...

or spotty ...

or dangerously ill.

Doctors use drugs very carefully. When you need some medicine, they fill out a special form.

They write down your name and address,
the name of the medicine, and the dose
that you need to take.

You take the form to the chemist.

She checks it and gives you the
medicine you need.

Your name and the dose
are on the label.

Not every kind of drug needs a form from the doctor.

The chemist sells many in her shop.

19

Medicines are safe as long as we use them properly.

<u>Never</u> take a medicine that is not for you.

Lizzie Chapman - one spoonful three times a day.

A parent will help you take the proper dose.

There are different kinds of drugs
in the world around us.

Not all of them are
medicines. Cigarettes can
make people very ill, and are
nasty for everybody else.

Alcohol is a strong drink.

Too much of it makes people noisy
and frightening.

There are things in the home that are nasty, too, although they do very useful jobs.

Strong cleaners could harm you if you swallowed them.

Strong glues have a smell that can hurt your head, and make you feel really strange.

Some people do not look after themselves.

They take strong drugs that can damage their body.

Drugs like these don't make people better.

They only make them feel worse.

27

Your body is precious, but it can be easily damaged.

Never swallow things that might harm it.

You own your body.
You have to look after it.

TOPIC WEB

Maths
Using the example on p17, work out how much cough mixture Lizzy will take each day and how much in a week. Express each figure in spoonfuls.

Design and Technology
Design a poster showing unhealthy activities contrasted with healthy activities.

History
Find out how people coped with illnesses without modern drugs. Ask older people about which drugs were considered a problem in their day.

Science
Show on a picture of the body which part is affected by each of the illnesses and conditions mentioned in the book.

Geography
Find out about the access to health care in a locality in a poor country being studied. Can people get to a doctor and can they afford the medicines?

R.E.
Find out what different religions say about keeping the body healthy and the misuse of substances.

Language
Write about when you were ill, describing how you felt emotionally and physically, and how it felt to get better again.

Art and Craft
Draw the rooms in your home and show where medicines and household chemicals should be safely stored in each room.

Music
Find or make up a song about feeling ill, creating the relevant mood and accompanying it with suitable sound effects.

P.E./Dance/Drama
Develop a role play about someone misusing drugs, and the effects on their body.

GLOSSARY

asthma A condition that affects the tubes that go to the lungs.

diabetes A condition that means a person cannot make energy from sugars.

disease Something that can make the body ill.

dose The amount of medicine that should be taken at one time.

germs Tiny forms of animal or plant life – some which cause illnesses.

inhaler A device for breathing medicine into the lungs, through the mouth.

BOOKS TO READ

Drugs and your Health by Jillian Powell (Health Matters series, Wayland, 2002)

For slightly older readers. This book looks at the effects of drugs on your body.

I'm Happy, I'm Healthy! by Alex Parsons (Life Education series, Franklin Watts, 1996)

One book in a health care series suitable for key stage one.

Why Do People Take Drugs? by Patsy Westcott (Wayland, 2001)

One title in a series of books that deals with issues that affect children's lives.

INDEX